JBILE

The CRAFTY HANDS *Collection*

Rag Dolls
Salt Dough Models
Simple Projects in Patchwork
Face Painting & Fancy Dress

First published in English in Great Britain
1995 by Aurum Press Ltd,
25 Bedford Avenue, London WC1B 3AT

Translated by Lydia Darbyshire

English translation copyright © Aurum Press 1995

First published as
Petits Ouvrages en Patchwork
1992 by Éditions Fleurus,
11 rue Duguay-Trouin, 75006 Paris, France

Copyright © Éditions Fleurus 1992

A catalogue record for this book is available from the British Library

ISBN 1 85410 327 X

1 3 5 7 9 10 8 6 4 2
1995 1997 1999 1998 1996

Printed in Italy

The
CRAFTY HANDS
Collection

SIMPLE PROJECTS IN
PATCHWORK

Text and projects:
Catherine Grosshans

Photographs:
Mariane Hufschmitt

Aurum Press

INTRODUCTION

The patchwork we know today has developed from an ancient technique that is almost as old as man's earliest clothes. The process involves using left-over pieces of material either to make complete garments or to decorate worn places on favourite clothes.

Early settlers in North America used scraps of old clothes to make new garments and household furnishings, including the beautiful quilts that are now so well-known and collected.

Today, patchwork has become an art form in its own right. On the pages that follow you will find lots of small articles made from patchwork, ranging from pincushions to table runners. All the projects give you an opportunity to express your own creativity in terms of colours and patterns, and you can use whatever type and colour of material you want.

Whether you are a beginner or a more experienced needle-worker, you are sure to find something here that you will want to make. To help you choose, each project is marked with one, two or three stars (*). One star means that the project is suitable for a beginner, two stars mean that a little more skill is needed, and three stars indicate projects that are suitable for more experienced stitchers.

CONTENTS

*	Very easy
**	Easy
***	Difficult

BASIC
TECHNIQUES

TERMINOLOGY

Patchwork : Needlework done by stitching together pieces or patches of fabric.

Appliqué : The art of stitching decorative motifs, either as simple shapes cut as one piece or as more complex patterns created from several pieces, directly on to fabric.

Quilting : Padded material made from three separate layers. The top layer, which can be made from patchwork, appliqué or a combination of both, should always have sufficient spare fabric around the edge to turn under neatly. The middle layer is a piece of lightweight, synthetic wadding. The bottom layer, the lining, is a single piece of fairly lightweight fabric.

CHOOSING YOUR FABRICS

You can use almost any kind of material you wish. If you are planning to combine brand new material with material that has previously been used and washed, it is a good idea to wash the new material before you begin so that it doesn't shrink the first time you wash the finished article. Avoid colours that run. You can cut up worn or outgrown clothes, or you can use offcuts from dress-making. Little pieces of new material will give really stunning results.

Your choice of colour and the different textures you use are the two most important factors influencing the success of your projects. There is nothing to stop you using different colours and types of materials from the ones we used, and, in fact, just changing the colour will completely change the appearance of the finished article.

TEMPLATES

Cut out the templates from thin card. The seam allowances are not shown. Always number the templates.

Remember: unless specifically stated, templates are *not* shown actual size.

THE SYMBOLISM OF COLOUR

Black	= mysterious – used for contrast
Blue	= peaceful – fresh
Green	= calm – refreshing
Grey	= soothing – transitional
Orange	= lively – cheerful
Purple	= luxurious – ceremonial
Red	= warm – passionate
Violet	= calming – melancholy
White	= cold – light – purity
Yellow	= light – sunny

CUTTING OUT THE MATERIAL

Remember that seam allowances are not included in the instructions.

For patchwork
Place the fabric with the wrong side facing upwards. Place the template along the straight grain of the fabric. Use tailor's chalk or pencil to draw around the template, then cut out the shape, adding on a seam allowance of 5mm/¼in all round.

For appliqué
Place the fabric with the right side facing upwards. Draw around the template using a dark crayon on dark fabric and a light crayon or chalk on light coloured material. Cut around the outline, adding a seam allowance of 5mm/¼in all round. Cut a series of V-shaped notches all the way round.

MAKING UP

Patchwork
You can either use a sewing machine (straight stitch) or work by hand (back stitch). Take two cut-out pieces, place them right sides together and hold them in place with pins, making sure that the threads in both pieces are running in the same direction. Sew the pieces together along one side, using the chalk line as a guide. Leave the two corners free.

Appliqué
Crease the shape along the chalk or crayon line so that the notched edge is folded under and lies flat. Place the shape, right side upwards, on the right side of the base fabric and pin it in position. Use either a sewing cotton of the same colour as the cut-out shape or transparent thread to sew the cut-out in position, using tiny slip stitches.
Avoid using light coloured material on a dark background.

QUILTING

Use your sewing machine (straight stitch) or work by hand (back stitch) and use a fairly strong thread. Your stitches must be small and even. If you are quilting a piece of patchwork, the line of stitches should be about 4mm/⅛in from the seams. If you are quilting appliqué, stitch around the outline of the shapes.

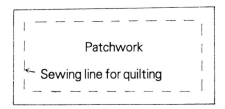

Patchwork
← Sewing line for quilting

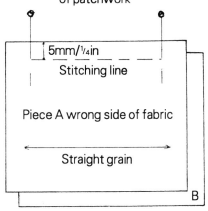

Stitching together two pieces of patchwork

5mm/¼in
Stitching line
Piece A wrong side of fabric
Straight grain
B

Stitching a piece of appliqué in position

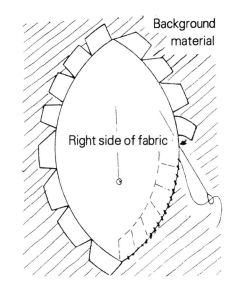

Background material
Right side of fabric

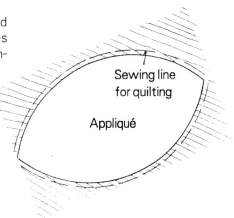

Sewing line for quilting
Appliqué

SEWING BAG

Difficulty **/Illustrated on page 9

YOU WILL NEED

Scraps of cotton in various colours
Cotton fabric, 6 x 21cm/2¼ x 8¼in for the base
Lining fabric, 30 x 35cm/12 x 14in
Wadding, 30 x 35cm/12 x 14in
Zip fastener, 28cm/11in
Bias binding, 60cm/24in

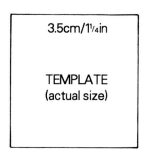

3.5cm/1¼in

TEMPLATE
(actual size)

MAKING UP

1. Cut out 64 squares, 3.5 x 3.5cm/1¼ x 1¼in, from the coloured cotton. Make the front by stitching 32 squares in four rows of eight squares. Repeat for the back. Press open the seams. Using the diagram below as reference, cut out the front and back.

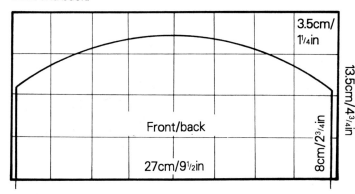

3.5cm/1¼in

Front/back

27cm/9½in

8cm/2¾in

13.5cm/4¾in

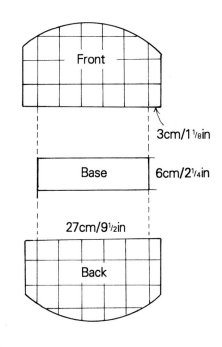

Front

3cm/1⅛in

Base

6cm/2¼in

27cm/9½in

Back

2. With wrong sides upwards, place the base between the back and front, so that it is 3cm/1⅛in from each end, as shown in the diagram. Stitch the back and front to the base.

3. With wrong sides upwards, place the wadding and lining fabric over the patchwork. Baste the three layers together so that they do not move while you work.

4. Working from the right side, stitch along the base seams and along the edges of each square to give a quilted effect. Trim the edges and remove the basting stitches.

5. Finish off the top edge with bias binding.

6. Turn the piece inside out, pin and stitch one side seam, sewing the base as shown in the diagram. Repeat at the other side. Oversew the inside seams.

7. Insert the zip fastener, finishing it off with a tassel.

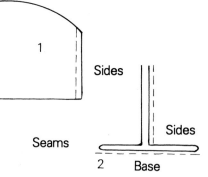

1

Sides

Sides

Seams

2   Base

SEWING KIT

Difficulty *\/Illustrated on page 9

YOU WILL NEED

Pieces of cotton in various colours
Wadding, 2 pieces, 30 x 15cm/12 x 6in and 10 x 15cm/4 x 6in
Lining fabric, 30 x 15cm/12 x 6in
Cotton fabric for pad, 9.5 x 11cm/3³/₄ x 4¹/₂in
Thick white flannel, 2 pieces, each 9 x 14cm/3¹/₂ x 5¹/₂in
Bias binding, 1.2m/4ft

MAKING UP

1. Using the template and adding 5mm/¹/₄in seam allowance all round each piece, cut out 40 squares, 2.5 x 2.5cm/1 x 1in, from the coloured cotton. Arrange them in 10 rows of four squares, stitching them together to form one piece. Press open the seams.

2. With wrong side upwards, place the wadding and the lining fabric over the patchwork. Baste the three layers together to stop them moving while you work.

3. From the front, oversew the seams of the squares to give a quilted effect. Trim the edges and remove the basting stitches.

4. Using the small piece of wadding and the small piece of cotton fabric, make a pad for the centre of the kit. Oversew it in place with tiny stitches.

5. Trim the edges of the two pieces of flannel with pinking shears. Fold each piece in two lengthways to form a four-page 'book', and use back stitch to hold them next to the pad to make a needle-holder.

6. Apply bias binding right around the outside edge.

7. Take two lengths of bias binding, each 15cm/6in long, and oversew the long edges together. Attach the ties to the front end and to the centre of the fourth row of squares as shown.

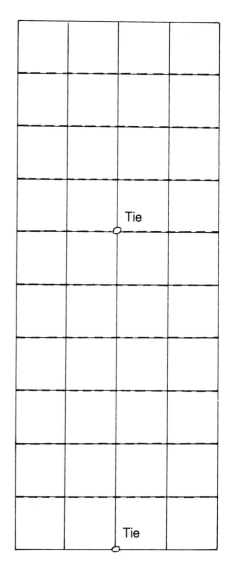

PINCUSHION

Difficulty ✱✱/Illustrated on pages 9 and 27

YOU WILL NEED

Scraps of cotton in various patterns
Card for templates
A piece of cotton, approximately
        30 x 15cm/12 x 6in
Clear, all-purpose adhesive
Polyester stuffing

MAKING UP

1.   From the card, cut five squares, each
3 x 3cm/1 ⅛ x 1 ⅛in, and four triangles, each
half one square. You will also need to cut a
piece of card that is the same overall dimensions
as the assembled squares and triangles (see diagram).

2.   Use the templates to cut from the cotton scraps five
squares and four triangles, adding 5mm/¼in seam allowance
all round each piece.

3.   Cut a long piece of fabric, 29 x 2cm/11 x ¾in, adding
5mm/¼in seam allowance, for the central band.

4.   Use the large template to cut out a single piece of fabric,
adding a seam allowance of about 1cm/½in all round.

5.   Assemble the patchwork pieces as shown in the diagram
and press the inside seams open.

6.   Stitch the long piece of material right around the outside
edge of the patchwork. This will give the pincushion the necessary depth. Close the side seam.

7.   Place the large cardboard template over the single piece
of material and cut a series of V-shaped notches around the
edge of the material. Fold over the notches and glue them
down. Leave until the adhesive is dry.

8.   Fill the top of the pincushion with polyester
stuffing. Attach the base to the bottom edge
of the centre band with tiny stitches, adding
more stuffing if necessary before finishing off.

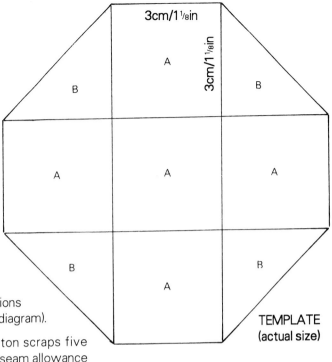

3cm/1 ⅛in

3cm/1 ⅛in

TEMPLATE
(actual size)

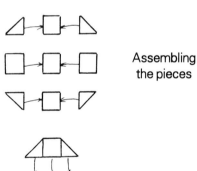

Assembling
the pieces

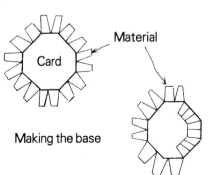

Material

Card

Making the base

11

ROUND PENCIL CASE

Difficulty ✳✳✳/Illustrated on page 13

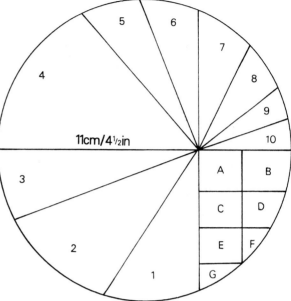

YOU WILL NEED

Card for templates
Pieces of coloured cotton material
Wadding, 40 x 20cm/16 x 8in
Lining fabric, 40 x 20cm/16 x 8in
Zip fastener, 18cm/7½in

MAKING UP

1.   On a piece of card, draw a circle with a diameter of 16cm/6½in and mark on it the outline of the patchwork as a guide to laying out the pieces. Cut out the templates from another piece of card; identify each template with a number or letter.

2.   Make the front from the patchwork pieces, using the templates as your guide and adding 5mm/¼in seam allowance all round each piece. Assemble the pieces as shown in the diagram and press open the inside seams.

3.   Make the back from a single piece of material. Cut out a circle 16cm/6½in in diameter, adding 5mm/¼in seam allowance all round.

4.   From the wadding and from the lining fabric cut two circles, each 17cm/7in in diameter. Baste one wadding and one lining circle to the front; repeat for the back.

5.   Oversew the lines of the patchwork on the front to give a quilted effect.

6.   Pin or baste the back and front pieces together, right sides facing, and stitch around the outside edge, remembering to leave 18cm/7½in gap for the zip fastener. Trim the inside edges and oversew them neatly. Remove the basting stitches and/or pins and turn the bag the right way out.

7.   Stitch the zip fastener into position.

8.   If you wish, decorate the front with novelty buttons.

Duffel-bag (page 14)
Round pencil case (page 12)

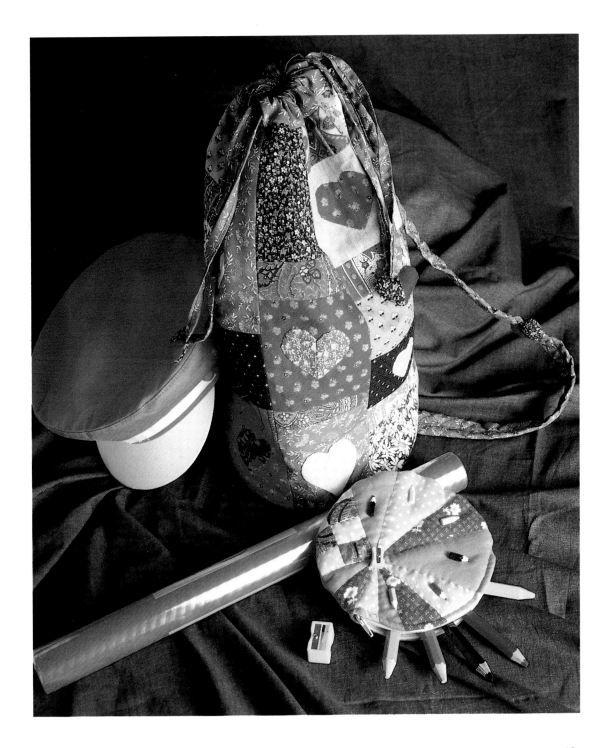

DUFFEL-BAG

Difficulty ✶✶/Illustrated on page 13

YOU WILL NEED

Quilted fabric, 75 x 50cm/30 x 20in
Pieces of coloured fabric
Card for templates
Small amount of polyester stuffing

MAKING UP

1. Adding 5mm/¼in seam allowance to all pieces, cut from the quilted fabric:
two circles, 17cm/7in in diameter, for the base;
one rectangle, 55 x 37cm/21½ x 14½in, for the lining;
one strip 70 x 6cm/27½ x 2½in for the strap.

2. From the pieces of coloured fabric, adding a seam allowance of 5mm/¼in to all pieces and using the diagram on page 15 as a guide, cut squares and rectangles to form a large rectangle 54 x 37cm/ 21 x 14½in. Also cut out two pieces, each 27 x 7cm/ 10½ x 2¾in, for the casement, and two pieces, each 60 x 2cm/24 x ¾in, for the ties.

3. Using the outlines on this page as a guide, cut templates for the hearts from card. Cut out a total of 13 large hearts and 7 small hearts from the coloured fabric.

4. When you are happy with the way you have arranged the squares and small rectangles cut in step 2, sew them together and press open the inside seams.

5. Assemble the hearts and appliqué them to the patchwork as shown in the diagram. Use tiny slip stitches and turn in the edges by 5mm/¼in all round.

6. With right sides facing, place the patchwork and lining fabric together. Baste together and stitch along the two short sides to form a cylinder. Trim and oversew the raw edges. Turn the right way out but so that the lining is on the outside.

7. With wrong sides facing, take the two circles for the base. Pin them together and baste them in position at the bottom of the cylinder. Stitch around the base, trim and oversew the raw edges. Turn the bag the right way out.

8. Make the casement from the two long rectangles cut in step 2. Turn in and hem the four short sides by 5mm/¼in. With right sides facing, place one long edge of one of the

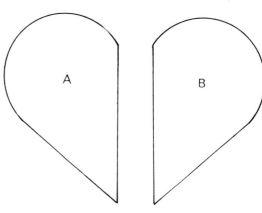

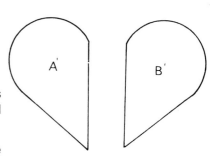

HEART TEMPLATES
(actual size)

37cm/14½in

9cm/3½in

BASE OF BAG

rectangles against the top edge of the bag. Stitch it in place, with a seam allowance of 5mm/¼in, so that your stitches go through both the patchwork and the lining fabric. Fold the rectangle to the inside and, turning in 5mm/¼in, hem along the inside, making sure that your stitches are not visible from the right side. Repeat at the opposite side of the bag top with the other section of casement.

9. Make two ties from the pieces cut in step 2, machine stitching the long edges of each piece and turning them right side out before pressing them flat. Thread one tie through both sections of the casement, bringing it back out at the side you started. Thread the other tie through the casement, but starting and finishing at the opposite side.

10. Attach two small hearts, sewn together and filled with polyester stuffing, to the free ends of both ties.

11. Make the strap, cut from quilted fabric in step 1, folding it lengthways, right sides facing, and stitching along the long edge. Turn it to the right side and press it carefully; it should be 3cm/1⅛in wide. Turn in the short ends and oversew neatly. Attach the strap to the bag, appliquéing a large heart to the bottom end and a small heart to the top. In the centre of the strap attach two small hearts, sewn together and filled with polyester stuffing (see the colour photograph on page 13).

Toilet bag (page 17)
Hearts & flowers (page 20)

TOILET BAG

Difficulty ✱✱/Illustrated on page 16

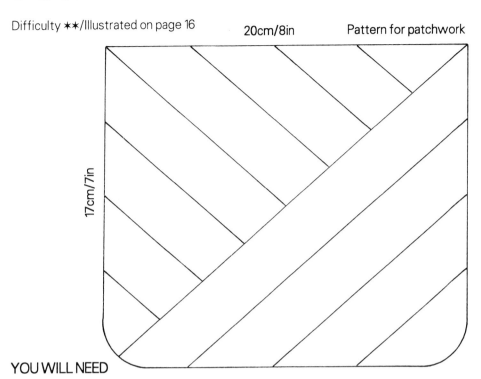

20cm/8in — 17cm/7in — Pattern for patchwork

YOU WILL NEED

Card for templates. Pieces of linen for the patchwork and 1 piece, 25 x 25cm/10 x 10in, for the back. Small pieces of contrasting fabric. Lace, 70cm/28in. Lining fabric, 50 x 25cm/20 x 10in. Wadding, 50 x 25cm/20 x 10in. Satin ribbon, 110cm/44in. Buttonhole cord, 10cm/4in. 2 buttons.

MAKING UP

1. Make the templates and cut out the patchwork pieces, the back and the lining, adding 5mm/¼in seam allowance to each piece. Complete the patchwork, stitching the lace in position as you work. Press the seams flat.

2. Cut the lining fabric and wadding in two and place a piece of wadding between the lining and the front. Baste the three layers together. Repeat for the back.

3. Stitch a length of ribbon along the top edge of the front, enclosing the raw edges. With the right sides outwards, sew the front and back together. Trim the edges neatly to the sewing line, then cover the joined edges with ribbon.

4. Attach two lengths of cord for the buttonholes then cover the top edge of the back with ribbon. Attach the buttons.

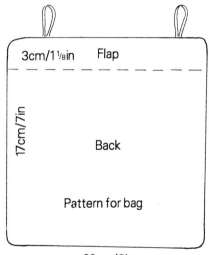

3cm/1⅛in — Flap — 17cm/7in — Back — Pattern for bag — 20cm/8in

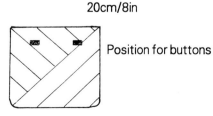

Position for buttons

MAKE-UP BAG

Difficulty ✱✱✱/Illustrated on page 19

Illustrated on page 19

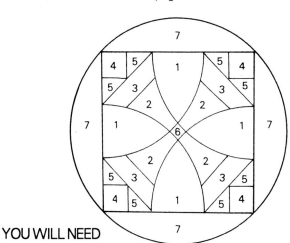

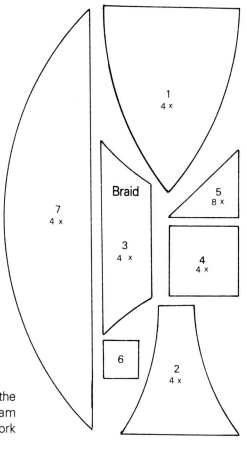

YOU WILL NEED

Card for templates
Scraps of material
Patterned braid, 30cm/12in
Wadding, 40 x 20cm/16 x 8in
Lining fabric, 40 x 20cm/16 x 8in
Zip fastener, 18cm/7½in
Pompon and tassel

MAKING UP

1. Copy the outlines of the templates onto card. Cut out the shapes in the fabrics of your choice, adding a seam allowance of 5mm/¼in all round. Assemble the patchwork and press open the inside seams.

2. Cut out a single piece of fabric for the back; you will need a circle 18cm/7½in in diameter plus a seam allowance of 5mm/¼in all round.

3. Cut out two circles from the wadding and two circles from the lining fabric, each circle 19cm/8in in diameter. Baste the front to a circle of wadding and a circle of lining fabric. Stitch along the seams of the patchwork.

4. Baste the back to a circle of wadding and a circle of lining, then place the back and front circles together, right sides facing. Stitch around the edge, leaving 18cm/7½in for the zip fastener. Clip and oversew the edges.

5. Turn the bag to the right side and insert the zip, attaching the pompon and tassel to the opener.

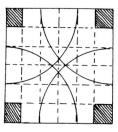

Cutting out guide

HEARTS & FLOWERS

Difficulty ✱✱✱/Illustrated on page 16

YOU WILL NEED

Stiff card for the base
Scraps of plain and floral-
    patterned fabric
Clear, all-purpose adhesive
Narrow satin ribbon
Card for the templates
Polyester stuffing or kapok
Embroidery cotton

MAKING UP

1.   Using the diagram on this page or
on page 21, transfer the outline of a
heart to the stiff card and cut out. Use
this to cut out a heart-shape from one
piece of fabric, leaving an allowance of
1cm/½in all round. Place the card in the centre of the
fabric and cut a series of V-shaped notches all the way
round the fabric. Glue the turned-over notches to the card
and glue a short length of satin ribbon to the centre top of the
base. Leave the adhesive to dry.

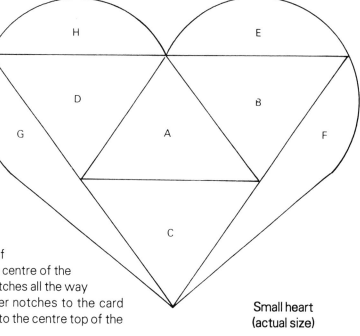

Small heart
(actual size)

2.   Prepare the templates for the front of the heart, and cut
out the shapes from patterned and plain fabrics, using the
colour photograph on page 16 as a guide and adding a seam
allowance of 5mm/¼in all round each piece.

3.   To make a small heart, cut out a strip of fabric 30 x 1cm/
12 x ½in, plus a seam allowance of 5mm/¼in all round. Make
up the patchwork and press open the inside seams. Attach
the strip to the front patchwork all the way round, then
attach it to the base, leaving a gap of about 4cm/1½in at one
side through which to stuff the heart. Close the gap with tiny
stitches.

4.   To make a large heart, attach the outer pieces of patchwork to the central heart (piece 13) in order. Press open the
inside seams. If you wish, embroider a row of chain stitches
around the edge of the inner heart and use tiny running stitches to embroider a name. Stitch the front patchwork to the
base, leaving a gap of about 7.5cm/3in at one side through
which to stuff the heart. Close the gap with tiny stitches.

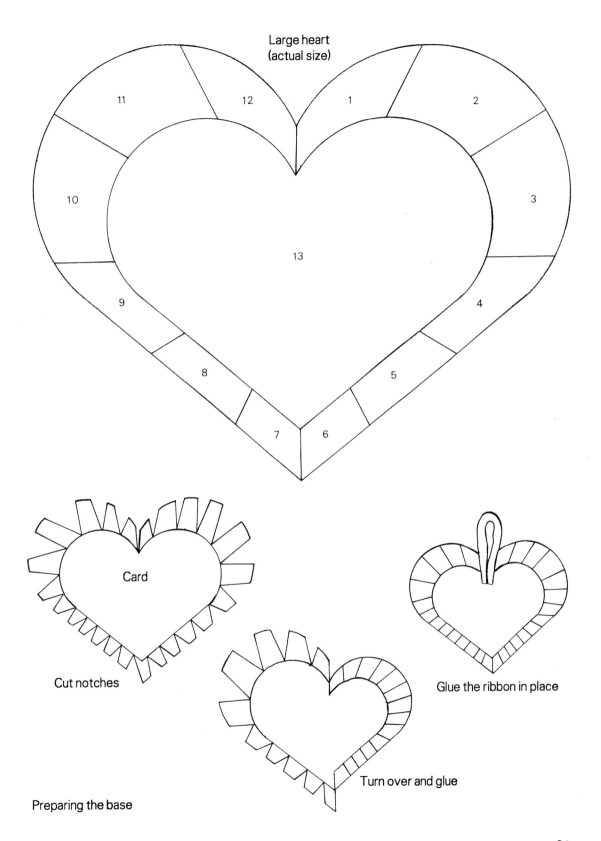

Large heart
(actual size)

11 12 1 2

10 3

13

9 4

8 5

7 6

Card

Cut notches

Preparing the base

Turn over and glue

Glue the ribbon in place

ZIPPED PURSE

Difficulty ∗/Illustrated on page 23

This useful little purse is very easily made in strips
of fabric mounted to make a band of patchwork.

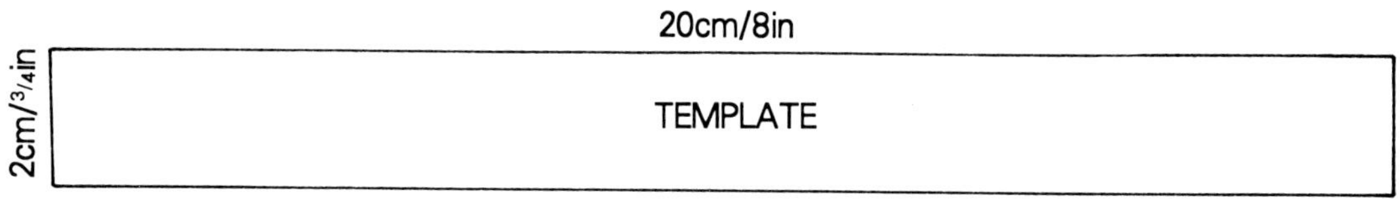

20cm/8in

2cm/³⁄₄in

TEMPLATE

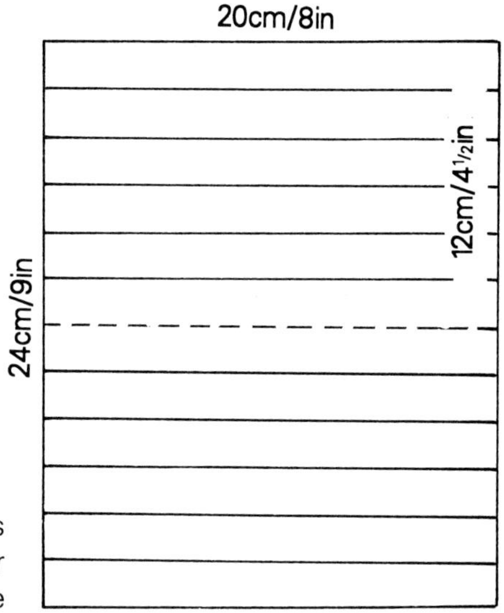

20cm/8in

24cm/9in

12cm/4¹⁄₂in

YOU WILL NEED

Pieces of fabric (at least 3 patterns)
Lining fabric, 26 x 22cm/10¹⁄₂ x 8¹⁄₂in
Wadding, 26 x 22cm/10¹⁄₂ x 8¹⁄₂in
Zip fastener, 20cm/8in

MAKING UP

1.   Cut 12 strips of material, each 20 x 2cm/8 x³⁄₄in, plus
5mm/¹⁄₄in seam allowance all round. Sew the strips together
to give a rectangle, 24 x 20cm/9 x 8in. Press open the inside
seams.

2.   Place the patchwork with the wrong side facing upwards,
and position on it the wadding and the lining material. Baste
the layers together and stitch along the seam lines. Remove
the basting stitches.

3.   Fold the rectangle in two, right sides together, and stitch
the two side seams. Clip the seams and oversew the edges.
Turn the purse the right way out.

4.   Insert the zip. If you wish, finish off the zip by adding two
small pieces of fabric, one to the zip opener and one to the
end of the zip but on the bag, so that you can hold the material
when you close and open the zip.

Hold-all (page 24)
Zipped purse (page 22)

HOLD-ALL

Difficulty ∗/Illustrated on page 23

YOU WILL NEED

Card for the template
Pieces of fabric (at least 3 patterns)
Lining fabric, approximately 65 x 35cm/25½ x 14in

MAKING UP

1. Cut a template, 5 x 5cm/2 x 2in, and use it to cut out 72 squares of fabric, remembering to add a seam allowance of 5mm/¼in all round each piece.

2. Assemble the squares to form a rectangle 12 squares deep by 6 squares across. Stitch the squares together and press open the inside seams.

3. Fold the finished patchwork in two, right sides together, and sew along the two side seams to create the bag. Trim and oversew the seams, then turn the bag right side out.

4. Make handles from two pieces of fabric, each 30 x 4cm/12 x 1½in. Sew each handle, right sides together, along the long edges, turn the right way out and press.

5. Cut the lining fabric to the size of the bag, 60 x 30cm/ 24 x 12in plus 5mm/¼in seam allowance all round, and fold it in two with right sides together. Stitch the two side seams together.

6. Turn down the top edge of the patchwork bag by 5mm/¼in and baste the hem in place.

7. Position the handles centrally, each end about 8cm/3in in from each side seam.

8. Place the liner inside the bag and turn down the top edge by 5mm/¼in all round. Baste it in position so that the top edge of the patchwork and the top edge of the liner align, with the handles between them. Stitch right around the top edge of the bag to hold the lining and patchwork together with the handles securely in place. Machine stitching is preferable for this stage if possible. Press lightly.

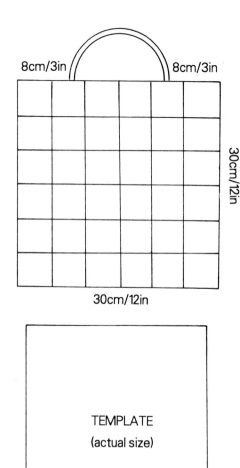

8cm/3in   8cm/3in

30cm/12in

30cm/12in

TEMPLATE
(actual size)

5cm/2in

DOLLY BAG

Difficulty ∗/Illustrated on pages 27 and 37

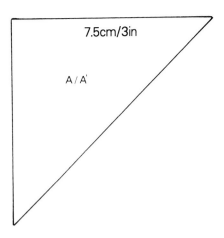

YOU WILL NEED

Card for the templates
Pieces of fabric (3 or more patterns)
Cord, 55cm/22in

MAKING UP

1. Cut a template for the triangles (piece A), then cut out 10 triangles, five of which should be in a strongly contrasting colour. You will also need: one strip of fabric (piece B), 37.5 x 3cm/14³/₄ x 1¹/₈in; one large rectangle (piece C), 37.5 x 25cm/14³/₄ x 10in; two circles, 12cm/4³/₄in in diameter for the base. Add a seam allowance of 5mm/¹/₄in to each piece.

2. Assemble the triangles as shown in the diagram. Press open the inside seams. Stitch pieces B and C along the bottom and top edges respectively of the triangles. The resulting rectangle should measure about 37.5cm x 35.5cm/14³/₄ x 14in. Press open the inside seams.

3. Fold the rectangle in two lengthways and, with right sides together, stitch along the long side seam to make a cylinder. Press open the seam.

4. Pin or baste the two circles for the base together, wrong sides together, and baste the edge of the base to the bottom edge of the cylinder, working with the cylinder the wrong way out and easing the fabric to fit neatly. Sew the base in position and remove the basting stitches and/or pins.

5. Still working from the inside, fold down the top half of the bag, turn under the seam allowance of the raw edge and stitch it into position around the base, covering the first seam. Turn the bag the right way out.

6. Measure a point 2.5cm/1in down from the top edge of the bag and a second point 1cm/¹/₂in down from the first. Work two parallel rows of stitches right around the bag from these points.

7. Make two buttonholes, at opposite sides of the bag, inside the rows of stitches. Cut the cord in half and, starting in one hole, thread the cord through the casement until it emerges through the same hole. Repeat with the other length of cord, but starting and finishing through the other hole. Finish off the cord with neat knots or tassels.

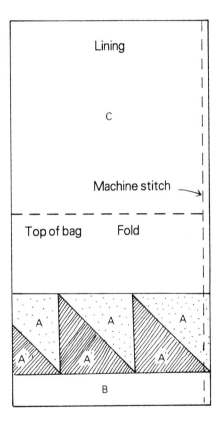

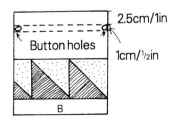

LAVENDER SACHETS

Difficulty ✳/Illustrated on pages 5, 27 and 31

These little sachets are an easy way to try out patchwork techniques. Here we show you twelve different motifs.

YOU WILL NEED

Card for templates
Tiny oddments of fabric; see the templates on pages 28–9
Narrow ribbon
Dried lavender

MAKING UP

1. Cut out of card the templates for the design of your choice and transfer the outlines to the fabric. Cut out the pieces, adding a 5mm/¼in seam allowance round each piece.

2. Assemble the patchwork, using pins to hold the separate pieces together while you work. Stitch the finished patchwork to a small rectangle, 8 x 6cm/2¾ x 2¼in, plus 5mm/¼in seam allowance, to make the front of the sachet.

3. Two of the patterns – the cube and the flower – are appliquéd directly to a piece of fabric measuring 14 x 8cm/5½ x 2¾in, plus 5mm/¼in seam allowance.

4. To complete the sachet, cut a piece of fabric for the back, 14 x 8cm/5½ x 2¾in, plus 5mm/¼in seam allowance, and place it, right sides together, on the front of the sachet.

5. Stitch the two long sides and the bottom edge together, leaving the top open. Turn the bag the right way out, fill with dried lavender and fasten with a length of ribbon.

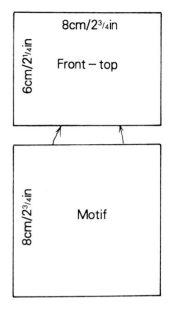

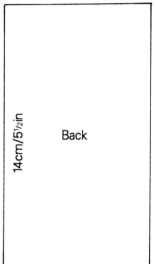

Fir tree motif

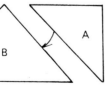
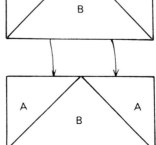
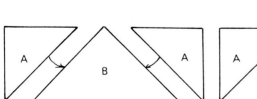
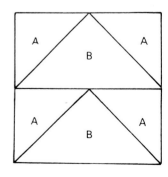

Dolly bag (page 25)
Lavender sachets (page 26)
Pincushion (page 11)

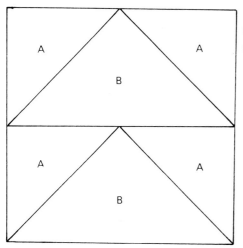

FIR TREE
(illustrated
on page 31)

PATCHES
(illustrated
on page 31)

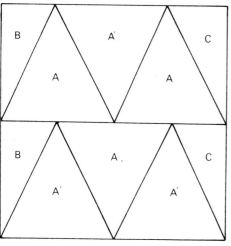

TRIANGLES
(illustrated
on page 5)

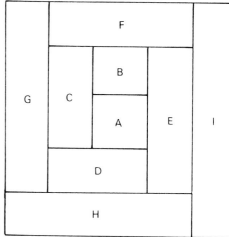

LOG CABIN
(not illustrated)

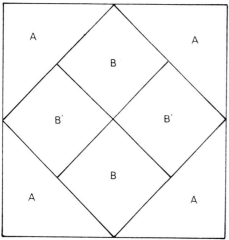

SQUARES
(illustrated
on page 27)

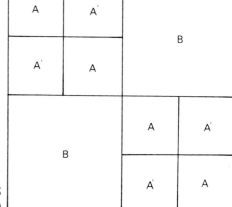

CHEQUERS
(not illustrated)

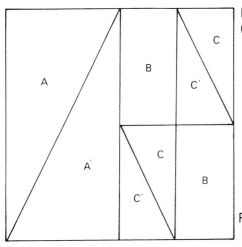

BUTTERFLY
(not illustrated)

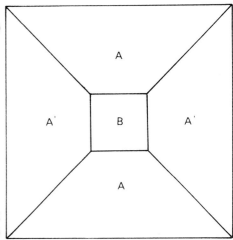

PERSPECTIVES
(not illustrated)

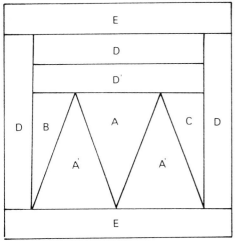

GEOMETRIC
(illustrated
on page 27)

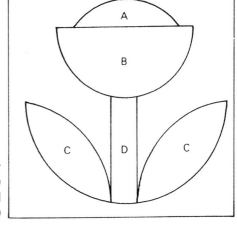

FLOWER –
appliqué
(illustrated
on page 27)

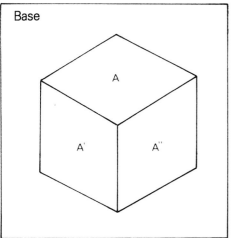

CUBE –
appliqué
(illustrated
on page 27)

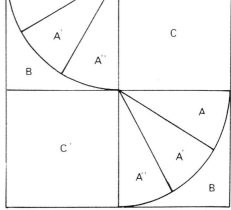

FANS
(not illustrated)

29

CHRISTMAS TABLE RUNNER

Difficulty **/Illustrated on page 31

YOU WILL NEED

Card for templates

Sufficient material to give overall dimensions of 77 x 21cm/
30 x 8¼in (we used pieces of plain white, red and green,
white with green fir trees, red with green fir trees and
green with red fir trees)

Cotton backing fabric, 80 x 25cm/31½ x 10in

Red bias binding, 2m/6ft

MAKING UP

1. Using the diagrams on this page as a guide, cut out templates from card. Transfer the outlines to the fabrics of your
choice and cut out the pieces, adding a seam allowance of
5mm/¼in all round.

2. Assemble the three star pieces, first into bands, then into
squares, using the guide below. Press open the inside seams.

3. Join the patchwork pieces with strips of fabric as shown
in the diagram.

4. Cut out four holly leaves (piece E) and appliqué them to
the corner squares of the central patchwork.

5. Cut off the corners of the four outermost squares (see
diagram), then pin and baste the patchwork to the backing
fabric, trimming this to size. If you wish, stitch through the
seam around the central square (piece A) of each patchwork.

6. Finish off by stitching bias binding over the raw edges all
the way round the runner.

Assembling the star   **Finishing off**

E
Actual
size

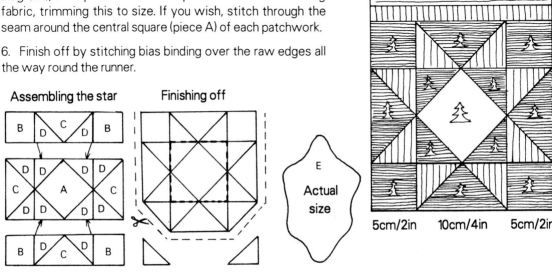

Christmas table runner (page 30)
Lavender sachets (page 26)

TRIANGULAR PINCUSHIONS

Difficulty ✶✶/Illustrated on pages 33 and 45

YOU WILL NEED

Card for templates
Scraps of fabric
Polyester stuffing
Glass beads or tiny weights for ballast
Tassels, pompons, buttons etc. for decoration

TEMPLATES

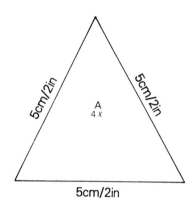

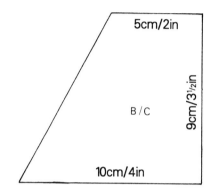

Assembling the patchwork

MAKING UP

1. Cut out the templates from card and transfer the outlines to the fabric. Cut out the pieces, adding a seam allowance of 5mm/¼in all round each one.

2. Assemble the patchwork as shown in the diagram. Press open the inside seams.

3. Fold the finished patchwork in two, right sides together, and stitch along two seams (see diagram).

4. Turn your work the right way out and insert the stuffing, adding the weights at the end, so that they stay near the bottom of the finished pincushion.

5. Bring corner 2 to corner 4, and use tiny stitches to over-sew the bottom seam, turning in 5mm/¼in along both edges.

6. Sew a button, tassel or pompon on the top.

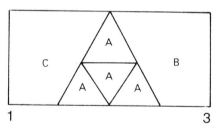

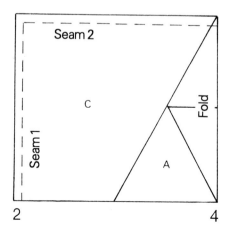

EVENING BAG

Difficulty ✱✱✱/Illustrated on front cover

YOU WILL NEED

Card for template
Pieces of coloured and patterned fabric for the motif
Black velvet, 70 x 50cm/28 x 20in
Lining fabric, 60 x 25cm/24 x 10in
Interfacing, 60 x 25cm/24 x 10in
Wadding for the motif, 15 x 10cm/6 x 4in
Zip fastener, 30cm/12in
Strip of black velvet for the strap, 117 x 6cm/46 x 2¼in
4 buttons

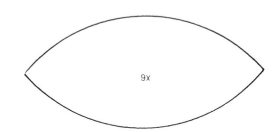

MAKING UP

1. Cut a template from card and cut out nine pieces from coloured fabric, adding 5mm/¼in all round each piece.

2. From patterned fabric cut two strips, each 25 x 5cm/ 10 x 2in, and one strip 20cm/8in long and about 5mm/¼in wide, adding a seam allowance of 5mm/¼in to all edges.

3. Using the diagram as a guide, transfer the outline of the bag to card and cut out two pieces, the back and the front, from the velvet, the lining and the interfacing.

4. Appliqué the ovals to the centre front of the bag, pinning each one in place and adding a little wadding behind it. Trim off excess material. Stitch around the edge of the completed motif. Appliqué the two broad strips and the narrow strip to the front of the bag.

5. Baste the interfacing to the front and back pieces of the bag, then stitch the zip fastener in place.

6. Turn the velvet right sides facing, open the zip and stitch around the sides and base of the bag. Turn the bag right way out.

7. Baste the lining pieces together, right sides facing, and stitch along the sides and across the bottom. Place the lining inside the bag, turn in the raw edges and slip stitch the lining to the zip fastener.

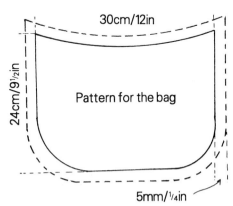

8. With right sides facing, fold the strip of velvet for the strap lengthways and stitch it together. Turn the strap the right way out and turn in and hem the two short ends.

9. Attach the strap to the sides of the bag, sewing on two buttons at each side for decoration. If you wish, twist the strap around black cord.

PAN HOLDERS

Difficulty **/Illustrated on page 37

YOU WILL NEED

Card for the templates
Pieces of fabric (3 different patterns)
Wadding, approximately 18 x 18cm/7½ x 7½in
1 square of plain fabric for the base, approximately
    18 x 18cm/7½ x 7½in
Bias binding, approximately 70cm/27½in

MAKING UP

1. For the Churn-dash pattern you will need 17 pieces as shown in the diagram below. Cut out the templates and use them to cut out the fabric, leaving seam allowances of 5mm/¼in all round. Cut four triangles (A) patterned fabric 1; four squares (B) plain fabric 2; four triangles (C) patterned fabric 3; five squares (D) patterned fabric 3.

2. Assemble the pieces as shown in the diagram. Press open the inside seams.

3. Pin and baste wadding between the finished patchwork and the fabric for the base, holding the three layers together while you stitch over the seams of the patchwork. Remove the pins and basting stitches and trim the edges.

4. Cover all the raw edges with bias binding.

TEMPLATES

3cm/1¼in
(actual size)
B

3cm/1¼in
(actual size)
D

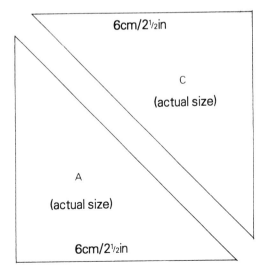

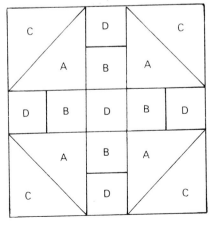

Fair and Square

You can make the Fair and Square pattern, which requires 13 pieces, from the diagram below. Follow the instructions for the Churn-dash pattern.

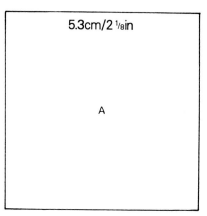

5.3cm/2 ⅛in

A

3.8cm/1½in

C

TEMPLATES

(actual size)

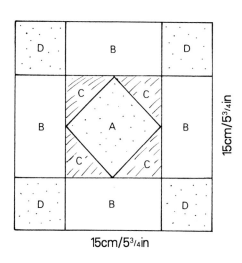

15cm/5¾in

15cm/5¾in

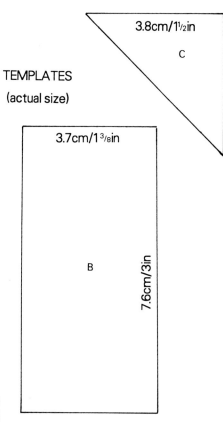

3.7cm/1 ⅜in

B

7.6cm/3in

Many other patchwork designs can be adapted for use in this way, and these are ideal projects for beginners. Make sure you use good quality cotton for the patchwork and base and thick wadding to protect your hands from the heat.

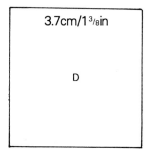

3.7cm/1 ⅜in

D

Dolly bag (page 25)
Pan holders (page 35)

LOG CABIN BAG

Difficulty **/Illustrated on page 41

We used a mixture of denim and brightly patterned fabrics for this bag. It's a good way of using up leftovers. Log Cabin is a traditional North American motif.

YOU WILL NEED

Card for the templates
Offcuts of patterned, lightweight fabric
White cotton fabric, 70 x 50cm/27½ x 20in
Denim, 120 x 50cm/48 x 20in
Quilted lining fabric, 70 x 50cm/27½ x 20in
Petersham ribbon for handles, 1m/3ft

MAKING THE LOG CABIN PATCHES

1. Cut out the nine templates from card, then cut out the nine pieces in the fabrics of your choice, adding a seam allowance of 5mm/¼in all round each piece.

2. This type of patchwork is made by starting with the central square (piece 1) and attaching rectangles around the square, in the order shown in the diagram. Turn the piece in a clockwise direction as you work until you have added the final rectangle (piece 9), giving a square of about 10 x 10cm/ 4 x 4in plus the 5mm/¼in seam allowance left all round. Press open the seams.

3. Sew the completed motif onto a base of white cotton, 12 x 12cm/4¾ x 4¾in. You might find it helpful to draw the outline of the design on the cotton before you begin, as a guide while you work.

4. Make a total of 12 motifs in a variety of patterns and colours.

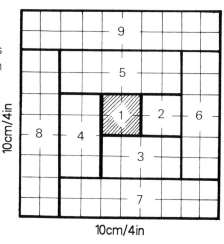

10cm/4in

10cm/4in

Assembling the motif

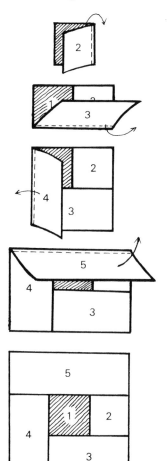

etc...

38

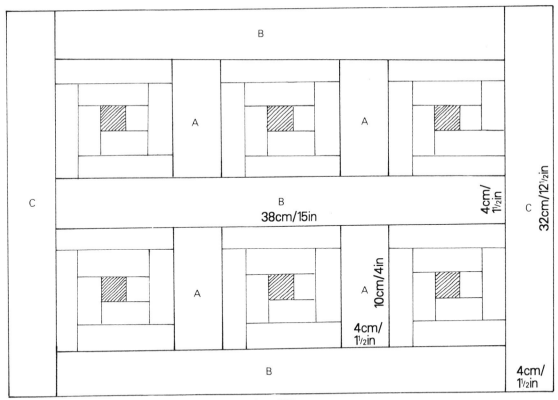

B

A · A

C · C

4cm/ 1½in

32cm/12½in

B
38cm/15in

10cm/4in

4cm/ 1½in

A · A · A

4cm/ 1½in

B

4cm/ 1½in

46cm/18in

MAKING UP THE BAG

1. Cut out templates for the bag from card, using the diagram as a guide. Use the templates to cut from the denim the following pieces: eight strips (A), each 10 x 4cm/4 x 1½in; six strips (B), each 38 x 4cm/15 x 1½in; and four strips (C), each 32 x 4cm/12½ x 1½in. You will also need a strip, 120 x 10cm/48 x 4in, for the base and sides of the bag. Remember to add 5mm/¼in seam allowance to all the pieces.

2. Assemble, as you would for a patchwork, the six completed Log Cabin motifs and the strips of denim. Repeat with the remaining motifs and strips. Press open the seams.

3. Attach the strip cut for the base and sides.

4. Cut from the quilted lining fabric two rectangles, each 46 x 32cm/18 x 12½in, and a strip, 120 x 10cm/48 x 4in. Remember to add 5mm/¼in seam allowance all round all the pieces. Stitch the pieces together.

5. Place the lining inside the bag and turn the top raw edges inwards. Stitch the lining in position around the top of the bag.

6. Cut two handles from the ribbon and attach them securely as shown in the colour photograph on page 41.

GAMES BAG

Difficulty *∕Illustrated on page 41

YOU WILL NEED

Card for templates
Pieces of fabric (4 colours)
Base fabric, approximately 70 x 42cm/27½ x 16½in
Lining fabric, approximately 70 x 42cm/27½ x 16½in
Tape or **cord,** 60cm/24in
Embroidery cotton

MAKING UP

1. Transfer the outlines of the motif to card and cut out the templates. Cut the pieces from coloured cotton, adding a seam allowance of 5mm/¼in all round each piece.

2. Assemble the patchwork as shown in the diagram. The finished piece should measure about 12 x 10cm/5 x 4in. Press open the seams. You will probably find it easier to embroider a name on this section at this stage (see colour illustration).

3. Cut out from the base fabric four pieces (one 20 x 20cm/8 x 8in; two 10 x 4cm/4 x 1½in; one 20 x 4cm/ 8 x 1½in) plus seam allowances, and assemble them, with the patchwork, to give an overall rectangle for the front of the bag of about 34 x 20cm/13½ x 8in. Cut a second rectangle to the same dimensions for the back.

4. Cut out two pieces of lining fabric, each about 34 x 20cm/13½ x 8in, plus 5mm/¼in seam allowance.

5. Place the front on a lining piece, wrong sides together, and pin then baste together. Repeat with the back. With right sides together, place the front and back sections together and stitch across the base and down both sides, leaving a gap of about 2cm/¾in at one side about 2.5cm/1in down from the top. Trim and oversew the edges.

6. Turn in the raw edges at the top, and slip stitch the lining in place around the top edge.

7. Using the hole in the side as a position guide, run a row of stitches right round the top of the bag, below the hole and about 4cm/1½in down. Thread cord or tape through the casement thus formed.

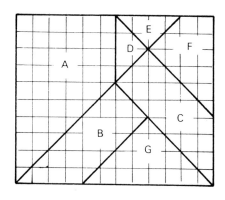

TEMPLATES

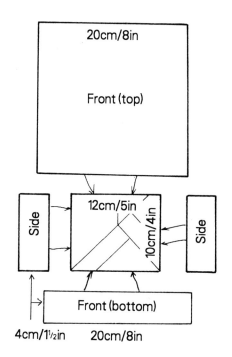

Log Cabin bag (page 38)
Games bag (page 40)

PLACE MATS

Difficulty **/Illustrated on page 5

YOU WILL NEED

Card for templates
Pieces of cotton fabric (2 patterned, 1 plain)
Material for the base, approximately 45 x 35cm/18 x 14in
Bias binding, 1.5m/5ft

MAKING UP

1. Transfer the templates to card and use them to cut the following: six squares (A) patterned; two squares (A') plain; six large triangles (B) plain; four small triangles (C) plain. You will also need to cut four edging strips, each 30 x 5cm/11½ x 2in. Remember to add 5mm/¼in seam allowance all round each piece.

2. Assemble the centre of the patchwork as shown in the diagram, and then add the side pieces. Press open the seams.

3. Place the finished patchwork on the backing fabric and pin, then baste it in position. Trim the backing to size.

4. Cover the edges with bias binding.

5. If you wish, you can stitch along the seam lines of the patchwork section, through to the base.

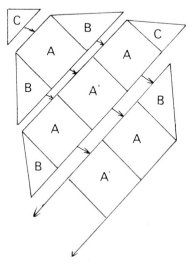

Assembling the patchwork

TEMPLATES (actual size)

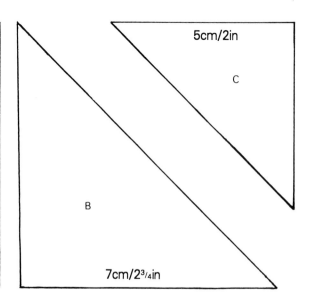

7cm/2¾in

A/A'

5cm/2in

C

B

7cm/2¾in

30cm/11½in

5cm/2in

5cm/2in

C

B

C

B

A'

B

30cm/11½in

40cm/15½in

B

A'

B

C

B

C

43

NAPKIN HOLDERS

Difficulty ✶✶/Illustrated on pages 5 and 45

YOU WILL NEED

Fabric for each holder, 38 x 27cm/15 x 10½in
Card for templates
Pieces of material for the motifs

MAKING UP THE HOLDER

1. Turn up and stitch a hem of 1cm/½in along one of the short ends (section 1).

2. Turn over the material and fold up the bottom, hemmed third (section 1) so that it is over the central third (section 2) with right sides together. Stitch the two side seams, leaving 1cm/½in seam. Turn the right way out.

3. Turn in a hem of 1cm/½in all the way around the flap. Press lightly.

ADDING THE MOTIF

1. Whatever style or pattern of decoration you choose (see diagrams below and on page 46 for some ideas), transfer the templates to card and cut out the pieces, adding 5mm/¼in seam allowance around each piece.

2. Assemble the patchwork and appliqué it to the flap of the holder.

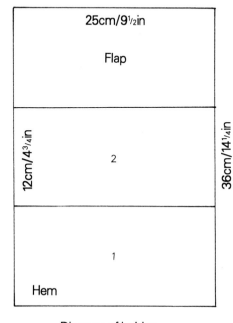

Diagram of holder

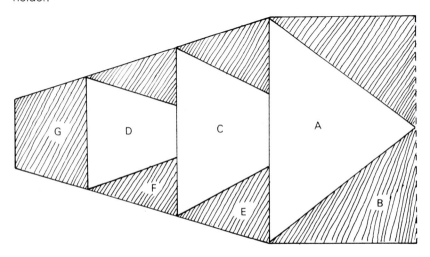

Half arrow-head motif
(actual size)

Napkin holders (page 44)
Triangular pincushion (page 32)

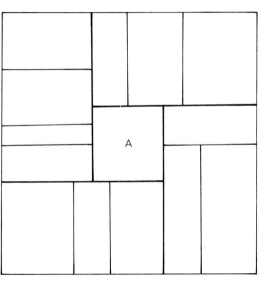

Motifs
(actual size)

Illustrated on page 45

Illustrated on page 45

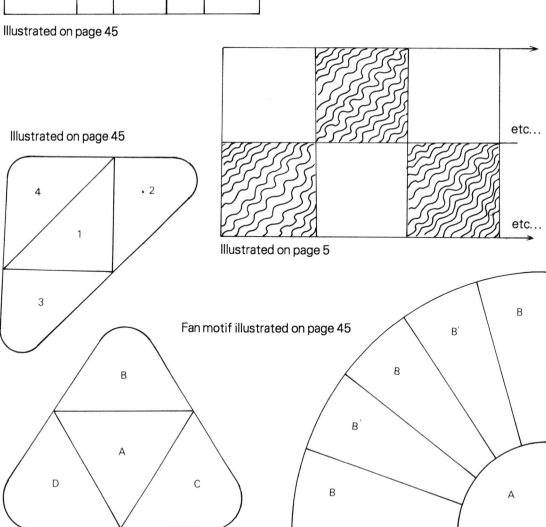

etc…

etc…

Illustrated on page 5

Fan motif illustrated on page 45